MW00718863

Stretch Marks

Devotions for the Not-So-Perfect Woman

Gloria McQueen Stockstill

CROSSBOOKS

CrossBooks™
A Division of LifeWay
1663 Liberty Drive
Bloomington, IN 47403
www.crossbooks.com
Phone: 1-866-879-0502

First published by CrossBooks 04/18/2012

ISBN: 978-1-4627-1416-2 (hc)
ISBN: 978-1-4627-1415-5 (sc)
ISBN: 978-1-4627-1414-8 (e)

Library of Congress Control Number: 2012902192

Printed in the United States of America

This book is printed on acid-free paper.

Any people depicted in stock imagery provided by Thinkstock are models, and such images are being used for illustrative purposes only.

Certain stock imagery © *Thinkstock.*

Also by Gloria McQueen Stockstill

Family on the Rock, Or How to Keep Your Family off the Rocks
(with Wayne Stockstill)

Forty Days Toward Spiritual Maturity (with Wayne Stockstill)

- Listen! Look! Series (Concordia Publishing House):
- The Basket in the River (English and Spanish)
- To the Town of Bethlehem (English and Spanish)
- Jesus Rose on Easter Morn (English and Spanish)
- The Blind Man by the Road (English and Spanish)

To my husband, Wayne. Your support of my writing ministry has never faltered. For that, I am grateful!

To women of all shapes, sizes, and colors. I hope you realize how precious you are in God's sight. I want you to know you may lead ordinary lives but, because you are created in the image of God, that makes you extraordinary. That's the only kind of extraordinary that really matters!

"You grow up the day you have your first real laugh—at yourself."

Ethel Barrymore

Contents

Preface

This book began as a blog. Each day I would bemoan how aging was affecting me or reveal some outlandish thing I had done during the week. God always gave me a spiritual application for my posting.

I admit there were times I said, "God, how are you possibly going to get a spiritual truth out of this?" Ever faithful, He placed in my mind and heart a truth that tied together with what had happened or how I was feeling.

The book shows how God reveals spiritual truths, even in situations that seem ridiculous. It also shows that God speaks to ordinary people, people who are not great scholars, not great theologians, and not great preachers. He is willing to speak to you, too. The key is to be listening!

I pray this book will both encourage you in your spiritual walk with the Lord and give you a good laugh as well. After all, God did say laughter was good medicine!

Gloria McQueen Stockstill

Acknowledgments

To God, who gave me any writing ability I might have. He has blessed me with something that brings me delight beyond measure. I love writing like I love breathing. Okay, I could do without the writing better than the breathing, but much of the joy in my life would be missing if I could not write. I am so grateful He determined I should be a writer!

When I first felt God leading me into the writing field, my husband was my greatest supporter. After ten years, he is still lending support and encouragement. That is most important to me.

Thanks to my daughter, Cynthia Stockstill Rodi, who spent many hours working with me on editing this book. Her efforts are greatly appreciated. It was fun to work with her. I hope someday we will write books together (hint, hint).

Thanks to my family for cheering me on. I'll always remember when my grandson, Caleb, called to tell me the family had seen my books advertised in a bookstore publication. They were more thrilled than I was. You can't beat that kind of encouragement!

Many thanks to Nancy I. Sanders, my mentor for the ten years I've been writing. I have learned so much from her, and no one could be more encouraging.

Thanks to my critique group, Wordsmiths. Through the years, these Wordie Sisters have helped me in honing my craft. I could not have done it without them!

Introduction

Most women don't look like the Hollywood beauties on movie screens or the pencil-thin models seen in the pages of magazines. Ordinary women struggle with weight. Ordinary women may not look stunning, even after putting on their makeup. Ordinary women find it difficult to get everything done in a twenty-four-hour period. Ordinary women may leave their beds unmade for one, two, maybe even three days at a time. Ordinary women's marriages are not perfect, and neither are their kids.

Stretch Marks: Devotions for the Not-So-Perfect Woman was written for the ordinary woman. My hope is that, when she reads it, she'll laugh aloud because she sees herself in the stories. I also hope she will realize God can speak to her in her ordinary, not-so-perfect life.

Forty Days of
Daily Devotions

Mismatched Knee-Highs

Yesterday, I stood on the platform before our congregation *three times* and never knew I was wearing mismatched knee-highs. It was not until I got home from church and slipped my legs out of the car that I realized I had on one patterned and one plain knee-high.

I wondered if I could convince people I really meant to do that; kind of like a new fashion trend. With what I see as fashion today, I don't think it's too farfetched!

I had to tell my friends. I don't know why I don't keep my mouth shut about such things. That way everyone would think I'm a suave, sophisticated intellectual who has an *all-together* lifestyle. Actually, I don't think anyone who knows me would buy that!

Some Christians live mismatched lives. They've been chosen by God to be His children. On one hand, they try to do what God wants. On the other, they want to do things that are contrary to what God teaches.

When we allow things into our lives that do not match his character or what He would do, we become mismatched Christians.

Check it out. Are you living a mismatched life? Do you need to add or eliminate things that will make you "match" your Savior?

Hoping I'm not a mismatched Christian,

Gloria

Something to Think About

If you live a mismatched life, can you really ever have the abundant life God wants for you?

Prayer

God, reveal to me when I am living a mismatched life.

Amen.

My Thoughts

Can You Hear Me Now?

A friend called me on my cell phone the other day. I couldn't hear her very well. When we were finished talking and I turned off my cell phone, I realized why I could not hear her: I had the phone upside down!

I called her back and told her what I had done, and we had a good laugh at my expense. Funny, my friends are always having a good laugh at my expense.

I wonder if sometimes we cannot hear God because we're trying to listen the wrong way. Maybe we fail to hear what God is saying because we're too busy demanding things from him or telling him how we think He should work things out.

It's really hard to hear someone else when you're so busy talking. It's kind of like having the phone upside down.

We need to turn the phone around so we can hear him clearly.

Hoping I'm listening to God the right way,

Gloria

Something to Think About

When you pray, do you talk more than you listen?

Prayer

God, I do tend to have my prayer life upside down. Help me be quiet and listen to what you want to say to me.

Amen.

My Thoughts

Spiritual Sunglasses

While riding in the car with my husband the other night, I was having difficulty seeing. I asked him if he had the headlights on. He said yes.

I replied, "You need to check the headlights. They aren't burning very brightly. That could be dangerous." He said he could see fine. Of course, he would say that.

I didn't say anything else but fretted that it was so difficult to see. It was not until we arrived home that I realized I had *sunglasses* on. No wonder I couldn't see!

When I told him what I had done, he only shook his head. He is seldom surprised at anything I do.

Sometimes we can have on spiritual sunglasses. They make it difficult to see where God is leading us. We may not even realize we have them on.

Ask the Holy Spirit to reveal if you are wearing spiritual sunglasses. He will show you. Then it's your responsibility to take them off.

Hoping I'm not wearing spiritual sunglasses,

Gloria

Something to Think About

Are you wearing spiritual sunglasses? When you do, it's difficult to see where God wants to lead you.

Prayer

God, reveal to me if I have on spiritual sunglasses. Help me be willing to take them off so I can clearly see where you want to direct my life.

Amen.

My Thoughts

Sin Squeakers

I stayed in bed this morning, not because I was asleep, but because I'm such a good wife. Well, at least I was today.

When I get out of our bed, it squeaks. We're not talkin' about a soft, little squeak but one that could wake the dead.

I knew if I got up, it would rouse my exhausted hubby, so I lay there . . . and lay there . . . and lay there.

When I could take it no more, I tried to get out as quietly as possible. It sounded like a groaning giant (I'm not referring to my size!) had awakened. So much for sleep!

It got me to thinking: what if God had us squeak every time we started to do something wrong? For example, if I start to open my mouth to say something unkind about another person, a loud squeak would come out instead. Not only God, but everyone near me would know I was about to say something wrong. Wow! I think that would make me use my tongue more wisely.

Or, if I'm sitting in a crowded room and think something ungodly, a loud squeak would emanate from me. Everyone in the room would know I have thought something wrong.

The more I think about it, God was wise not to do that. If there was a squeak every time someone did something wrong, there would be so many squeaks going off at once, we wouldn't be able to hear anything else. Talk about noise pollution!

I'm thankful God was so gracious as not to give us squeaks. He knows when we do wrong and expects us to confess it, but it's between Him and each of us. What an awesome God!

Thankful I don't have a sin squeaker,

Gloria

Something to Think About

Aren't you glad God gave us the Holy Spirit to reveal when we do something wrong instead of a sin squeaker?

Prayer

God, I thank you the Holy Spirit reveals to me when I start to do something that is unbecoming to who I am—a child of God.

Amen.

My Thoughts

Quitters Never Win

I just remembered something I read a long time ago. It said women in Hollywood who were—how do I say this kindly?—*getting along in years* were made to look younger with tape.

Yep, you read it right. The article said they took some kind of tape, pulled the wrinkles back toward the hairline, and, like magic, no more wrinkles!

Why didn't I remember that before? All this time I could have been wrinkle free and the envy of all my aging friends.

I got to thinking though: if I tape my face back against my hairline, I'll eventually have to change the tape. Won't the tape rip out what hair I have left? Do I want to be bald or wrinkle free? I guess I'll opt for wrinkles.

If the tape gets dirty, how do I clean it? If I don't clean it, people may shy away from me because they think I haven't taken a bath in weeks.

Drat! I guess tape is out. I thought I had the answer to my aging look!

Hey, I'm like Thomas Edison. I'll keep trying to think of an inexpensive way to hide the ravages of years. No quit in this girl.

I hope there is no quit in me when it comes to becoming more like Jesus.

I hope there is no quit in me when it comes to being compassionate and forgiving.

I hope there is no quit in me when it comes to considering others more than I do myself.

Wrinkles, I can live with. Quitting on the spiritual stuff . . . not a good idea!

Hoping I'm not a quitter,

Gloria

Something to Think About

Is it possible you have quit on some areas of your spiritual life?

Prayer

God, I've quit on some areas of my spiritual life. I yield to the Holy Spirit and ask you to help me get back on track and not be a quitter.

Amen.

My Thoughts

I Love a Good Ending

We were invited to a friend's birthday party. Since it was a warm day, I wore my *pedal pushers*. Most of you may not be old enough to know the term. It was a name for pants that were about calf high.

I showered, quickly got dressed, and we headed for the party. Out in the sunshine, I could see I had not remembered to shave my legs. I was not about to go to the party looking like Big Foot!

Since I had to stop at the store anyway, I grabbed a can of shaving cream and a pack of those cheap plastic shavers. While my husband drove, I shaved my legs.

What? You don't do that kind of thing? Hey, you do what you gotta do!

Except for a few nicks and a little blood oozing down my legs, you couldn't even tell what I had done. As they say, "All's well that ends well."

Endings are important in the spiritual world too. Believe in Jesus. Go to heaven. Good ending! Reject Jesus, eternal separation from God. Not a good ending!

I hope you have the same confidence I do that your life is going to end well.

Praising God I am confident of how it's going to end,

Gloria

Something to Think About

Are you confident of where you will spend eternity?

Prayer

God, thank you I can be confident of where I will spend eternity. Help me let others know about you so they can have that same confidence.

Amen.

My Thoughts

Cornmeal Shampoo

As I was getting ready for church, I realized I hadn't washed my hair.

I was dressed and not about to get back into the shower. I decided to resort to Plan B.

In my earlier years, if you didn't have time to wash your hair, you used white cornmeal to *wash* it. You just rubbed it through your hair and it absorbed the oil.

I went looking for white cornmeal. I could only find yellow. I had the option of using yellow cornmeal or going to church with very greasy hair. I opted for yellow.

I poured cornmeal on my head, rubbed it in, and shook my head. A cloud of yellow dust filled the bathroom. I looked down at my clothes. A line of cornmeal began at my blouse and ended at the bottom of my black slacks.

I also noticed a layer of yellow cornmeal encircling my shoulders. I wondered if the church members would just think I had yellow dandruff.

Pig Pen, the kid in the Peanuts cartoon, walked around in a cloud of dust. I'm sure he came to mind as I walked by church members. But my hair looked pretty good!

Maybe we put too much emphasis on what we look like when we go to church and not enough on why we are there, which is to worship and praise a magnificent God!

Hoping I concentrate on my heart and not my hair when I go to church,

Gloria

Something to Think About

When you go to church, is giving God the glory and praise He deserves your priority?

Prayer

Father, when I go to church, I don't want to let anything become more important to me than spending time worshipping and adoring you.

Amen.

My Thoughts

Preferences

Over or under? Which do you prefer? I'm talking about toilet paper here.

Do you put the toilet paper so that it rolls over the top or do you put it where it rolls under the bottom?

That may not sound like a big deal, but I once knew a couple who almost divorced because he was an under kind of guy and she was an over kind of gal. How could a person's preferences cause so much trouble?

I'm an over-the-top kind of girl myself. I have friends who are under-the-bottom types (although I can't imagine why). While I've been tempted to rearrange the toilet paper at their houses, I have, so far, had the discipline to refrain. After all, it is their preference.

Sometimes Christians have preferences.

"I prefer the King James Version of the Bible."

"I prefer hymns over praise music."

"I prefer the 9:30 service over the 11:00."

Toilet paper, whether over or under, accomplishes its purpose. So do different Bible translations, music, and times of services. We can't let our preferences be a means of causing dissension in the body of Christ.

Trying to not let my personal preferences cloud my godliness,

Gloria

Something to Think About

Is it possible you are allowing your preferences to cause dissention in God's church?

Prayer

Father, help me accept that others may not have the same preferences I do. Help me accept that we can use all our preferences to bring glory to you.

Amen.

My Thoughts

Words and *The Word*

I'm so old I've outlived words! How do I know that? Because a few days ago I went to get a yogurt and asked for nuts as a topping. After one bite, I said, "These nuts are rancid."

The young clerk looked at me as if I had just spoken a foreign language. I explained the word.

When is the last time you heard someone say, "He really is earnest"? The youth of today would probably think it was someone's name.

Or, how about "We're going to give the newlyweds a pounding"? It meant you gave them a pound of sugar, a pound of flour, etc. People today might think you were going to beat them up!

I went to the store recently and asked for Tempura so I could fry some shrimp. The young girl, who didn't look over ten, asked, "What's that?" So, between the chip and bread aisle, I gave her a detailed explanation about what it was and what you did with it. Her next question was, "Is it liquid?" I gave up and decided to grill the shrimp!

I may have outlived words, but I will never outlive God's Word, the Bible.

The Word of God is eternal, never changing. I have no fear its words will become archaic.

Jesus said, "Heaven and earth shall pass away, but my words shall never pass away" (Mark 13:31 KJV).

Thankful God's Word will never become obsolete,

Gloria

Something to Think About

Do you believe God's Word, the Bible, is still relevant, and that it is unchanging?

Prayer

God, help me believe the Bible is still as relevant today as it was when you inspired men to write it. Help me live my life according to what I read in its pages.

Amen.

My Thoughts

Open Doors

It's official: I am old! Can't be denied. I have cold, hard facts to prove it.

A woman opened a door for me. A not-so-young woman, at that.

If it had been a nice young man who opened a door for me, I would have thought, *Why, his mama surely did teach him how to be a gentleman.*

I tried to reason she was just being nice, but not even nice women open the door and wait for you to go in unless, of course, you're old!

The incident almost ruined my day. Lucky for my husband, I was able to drown my sorrow in a friend's coconut pie or I would probably have gone home, crawled into bed, and let my husband wait on his *old* wife. That coconut pie saved us both!

God opens doors. He opens doors to salvation, peace, joy, hope, and fellowship with himself. Those are doors you don't mind having opened for you, no matter what your age!

Thankful God has opened doors for me,

Gloria

Something to Think About

God will open doors for you. Are you willing to walk through them?

Prayer

Father, thank you for opening the doors of salvation, peace, joy, and hope. I pray I will walk through them all!

Amen.

My Thoughts

It Doesn't Take Much

Five words. That's all it took for him to make my day.

Did he say, "You've inherited five million dollars"? Was it, "I'm paying off your mortgage"? How about, "I'll publish all your books at my expense."?

Nothing that tremendous. He said, "You look three years younger."

I wish he had said, "You look ten years younger." But at my age, I'll take what I can get!

Kind words can change a person's day. They don't have to be life-changing words. They can be simple words like, "I hope you have a wonderful day." Or, "God bless you." Maybe, "God loves you."

A kind word may be just what a person needs to hear. This week, commit yourself to saying words of encouragement, praise, or kindness.

It can be at random places; at home, at school, at work, or at the grocery store. God could use your words to lift another person's spirit. And you may find it lifts yours, too.

Hoping my words lift spirits and encourage others,

Gloria

Something to Think About

Today, would you take the time and effort to share some kind words? The impact could be powerful.

Prayer

God, show me people who need to be encouraged and use my words to lift their spirits.

Amen.

My Thoughts

Waffles

I have the cleanest waffles in town. I can almost guarantee it.

I had my grandkids here for a few days. One was having a birthday so we decided to celebrate by having chocolate chip waffles for dinner.

We didn't eat them all so I put them in a plastic bag and saved them. I hoped they would want them for breakfast the next day since that would mean I didn't have to cook another big meal. I may be a devoted grandmother, but I still try to find ways to get out of cooking!

The next morning my hubby was taking the dishes out of the dishwasher. I heard, "What in the world?"

I rushed into the kitchen to see what had made him react. There in his hands was the plastic bag full of waffles. He had just pulled the bag out of the dishwasher! Now do you see why I said I have the cleanest waffles in town?

The plastic bag did a good job of keeping the waffles intact. In fact, I considered writing the company and telling them what their product was capable of doing. I hesitated only because I feared they would want me to tell my story on a television commercial. Then my ditsy tendencies would be known to millions. The thought made me a little queasy.

I can just see it. I'll be walking down the street and someone will stop me and say, "Hey, aren't you that ditsy lady who put your waffles in the dishwasher? Boy that was dumb."

I think I'll keep this between us. I'll tell people how sturdy the bags are without telling them how I know that.

One of the things I love about God is that He doesn't make us confess to everyone our stupid decisions, or our missing the mark.

He does want us to be willing to acknowledge them. His goal is not to shame us. He just wants us to be clean so our fellowship with Him isn't broken. Isn't that another indication of a loving God?

Thankful God has made me cleaner than my waffles,

Gloria

Something to Think About

God's goal is to make your life pure and clean. Is it yours?

Prayer

God, thank you for providing a way for me to be cleansed of my sins.

Amen.

My Thoughts

The Dance

I've invented a new dance. It's called, The Foot Stomp. This dance is not to be confused with a toe tapper.

A toe tapper means a song makes you want to tap your foot for the joy of the music. My dance is definitely not one of joy! The Foot Stomp dance is usually brought on by cramps in my feet.

The dance includes standing on my toes like a ballerina. It may also include jumping up and down while I try to press my feet through the floor.

The urge to do the Foot Stomp Dance can come on me at any time. It may be while I'm watching television. I just have to get up and dance. My husband doesn't think much of the dance when it obstructs his ability to watch a ballgame.

Sometimes the Foot Stomp Dance urge comes on me at 2:00 in the morning. I jump out of bed, run to the next room so as not to disturb my husband, and dance the dance.

I've even gotten the urge to do the Foot Stomp Dance while driving my car. It really is a challenge to do the dance and drive safely at the same time. I've been known to go a little faster as I push my foot down on the accelerator to rid myself of the pain.

I'm not sure the Foot Stomp Dance will catch on, but I believe there are many people who, although they do not know its name, know how to do it. Like me, they would be happy if they never did it again!

There is a dance I would like to see catch on. It's a dance unto the Lord. Psalm 149:3 says, "Let them praise him in the dance" (KJV).

Why not try it today. Lose all your inhibitions. Put some praise music on. Lift your hands to God in adoration. Sing along, if you like, *and dance!* The Lord will be delighted.

Hoping the only dancing I do today is unto the Lord,

Gloria

Something to Think About

Do you let your inhibitions keep you from praising and worshipping the Lord?

Prayer

God, help me have the courage to worship and praise you without any inhibitions.

Amen.

My Thoughts

Killing Your Friends

I had invited a few friends over for dinner. I decided to make brownies for dessert. Okay, if you want to get technical, Betty Crocker really made them. *But* I mixed them up and put them in the pan!

When I coated the pan so the brownies wouldn't stick, I noticed the spray smelled funny. I stuck my nose closer to the pan. This *was not* my Pam!

I went to the panty. There on the shelf, looking a great deal like my can of Pam was the Scott's Liquid Gold. For those of you who do not know, Scott's Liquid Gold is furniture cleaner!

I'm surely glad I wasn't so old I had lost my sense of smell. Having to rush your guests to the emergency room to get their stomachs pumped could really mess up a party!

People make mistakes all the time. Some have more serious consequences than others do. Even the ones we consider serious can be used by God to make us better. We just need to give them over to Him, ask forgiveness, and begin again.

Each day is fresh and full of potential. Following the Lord more closely will guarantee we don't make so many mistakes.

Thanking God He can turn things around, even when I mess up,

Gloria

Something to Think About

Are you letting what you have done in the past define your future?

Prayer

God, I often make mistakes. Thank you that you can even use my mistakes to make me into what you want me to be.

Amen.

My Thoughts

What's That in My Purse?

I have to be at church early since I lead in prayer at all the services. After the first service, I told my husband I was going to a fast-food place to get some breakfast and would be back in time for the second service.

I went to the restaurant and bought my breakfast along with a large Diet Coke. I slipped the drink into my purse and soon forgot it was there.

After the final service, I stood talking to one of our church members. She said, "Something is dripping all over my shoes. I think it's coming from your purse."

Sure enough, a steady flow of liquid originating from my purse was dripping onto her shoes.

I opened my purse to find a puddle of Diet Coke large enough to fill a small goldfish bowl. I apologized, but I'm sure she'll always check me for leaks!

My foremost thought as I dumped the soda out of my purse? What a waste of a Diet Coke!

I wonder if God ever says that about things.

"What a waste I have given them my Word and they don't even bother to read it.

What a waste I have promised to fellowship with them in prayer and they don't even bother to pray.

What a waste I have given them the privilege of sharing my gospel so I can add to my kingdom, but they don't bother sharing it.

Now those are *real* wastes!"

Hoping I don't waste opportunities God has given me,

Gloria

Something to Think About

Is it possible you are wasting opportunities? They can never be regained.

Prayer

God, I don't want to waste any opportunities you put before me. Help me be faithful to use every one you give me.

Amen.

My Thoughts

Cottonmouth Snakes

When my grandchildren come to the house, they love to watch nature shows on television. Usually we will see a snake slithering through the brush waiting to attack some poor creature or even a human who dares to cross its path.

I *hate* snakes. Live ones. Dead ones. Plastic ones. I despise them all. If I didn't love my grandchildren so much, I would not allow those shows to be seen in my house. High definition has only made it worse!

You may say, "It's only a picture." Hah! I've been known to break out in a sweat and have goose bumps the size of golf balls appear on my arms when a snake comes on the screen. The hair on my head stands so high I look a good two inches taller. Just writing about snakes makes me feel faint.

Someone shared a good illustration about snakes, if there is such a thing. He said some people are like the rattlesnake. It warns you it's about to attack by rattling its tail. Others are like the cottonmouth. It strikes without warning.

I would compare the Devil to a cottonmouth. He attacks when we least expect it. We're walking along life's path and *wham!* He appears out of nowhere, latching onto our flesh and causing us great pain.

We can't really prepare for the attack of a cottonmouth, but we *can* prepare for the attacks of the Devil. We must immerse our lives in all things godly. Become true disciples of Christ. Get to know Him and follow Him. The Devil may still attack but he'll find we have an impenetrable shield.

Thankful God can protect us from that snake, the Devil,

Gloria

Something to Think About

Do you know God has provided means to protect you against the Devil's attacks? You would be wise to use them.

Prayer

God, I want to defeat the Devil. Thank You for providing me ways to be victorious over him.

Amen.

My Thoughts

Hiding Things

I'm going to experience a trauma today. I'm going to the doctor.

The trauma is not really about the doctor but the fact that I'll have to get on the scales and someone will see how much I weigh. Even my husband doesn't know that!

I've debated about asking the nurse if she would leave the room. Even if I would promise to tell her how much I weigh, I doubt she would agree to do it.

When I'm going to the doctor, I dig through my closet to find the lightest clothes I own. Ditto for shoes. The wrong pair of shoes can add two or three pounds to the scale!

I always make my appointments for early morning and I *never* eat before I go. Don't want those eggs and bacon adding extra pounds!

Unlike when I go to the doctor, when I go into the presence of God there is no trauma. I don't have to hide anything. No need to try. He knows me better than I know myself! Yet, He still loves me. Totally awesome!

Thankful I don't need to try to hide things from God,

Gloria

Something to Think About

How do you feel when you go into the presence of God?

Prayer

God, I am amazed you see me as I am and still love me. I don't want to try and hide anything when I come into your presence.

Amen.

My Thoughts

Forgetfulness Has an Upside

I'd like to watch a movie and be able to discuss its great plot with people who loved it as much as I did. If they'll do it ten minutes after the movie, I can.

I'd like to remember where I left my purse a few hours earlier.

I'd like to know where my shoes are when I need them. I wouldn't bother looking in the closet. I *know* they won't be there.

I'd like to remember what I told my husband so he couldn't pull the old, "You just don't remember" card . . . although he's usually right!

I'd like to remember what I wore to church last Sunday so I don't have to ask my friends, "Did I wear this last week?"

Some positive things about being forgetful are these:

You fight less with your hubby. You can't remember why you were fighting!

You don't hold grudges because you don't remember when people do you wrong.

Since you can't remember the movies you watched, you're able to watch them over again, thus saving money.

The Bible says God forgets. He doesn't remember our sins against us. He does it, not because we deserve it, but simply because He chooses to do so.

Thankful God choses to forget my sins and not hold them against me,

Gloria

Something to Think About

Do you try to be forgetful about sins done against you? All of us would be better off if we were as forgetful as God.

Prayer

God, show me the things I need to forget and give me the grace to follow through.

Amen.

My Thoughts

Little Details Matter

My husband was getting ready for work and couldn't find a shirt . . . an ironed one that is.

I had three choices. I could convince him wrinkled shirts were *"in."* He's quite a smart man so I knew he wouldn't buy that one.

I could rush to a twenty-four-hour store and purchase a new shirt. Since I was low on cash, that wasn't an option.

The last resort was to iron a shirt. To my sorrow, I had to drag out the ironing board, wipe off the two-inch layer of dust, and start ironing.

I wondered why I had been so dumb as to buy a shirt that needed ironing. I guess it was because I had failed to look at the tag that said, "Iron on low." Not paying attention to that little detail was causing me great grief!

Personally, I think stores should make very large signs that say, "Buy this and you will spend hours at the ironing board." Since that would probably leave them with lots of *to-be-ironed* shirts they couldn't sell, I doubt that will ever happen. I guess I'll have to be more diligent about looking at those little details.

We need to pay attention to the little details in our spiritual life, too. It's not the big things that lead us away from God. It's the small things; using our tongue to slander someone, a wrong attitude, wanting our way no matter what—these are the things that harm our relationship with God.

Praying I am paying attention to the little details,

Gloria

Something to Think About

Are you paying attention to the *little* details in your spiritual life?

Prayer

Father, help me to pay attention to the little details that can hinder my relationship with you.

Amen.

My Thoughts

Patience Isn't Always Cheap

I was on my way to have lunch with my husband when I realized I had forgotten something. I drove back into the driveway and left the engine running and the car door open.

Once inside, I did something I seldom do. I decided to fix lunch!

I called my husband and told him to come home for lunch. After he got up off the floor, he said he would be home soon.

Thirty minutes later, he walked in and said, "How long were you going to leave the car running?"

The car! I had forgotten about it.

I was blessed that he came home for lunch. What if it had been dinner? The car might have been out of gas, and considering the cost of fuel, I don't think hubby would have been so patient. Just a guess.

I really am amazed at my husband's attitude, especially since these kinds of occurrences are ongoing. I doubt I would be as understanding.

I am also amazed at God's patience. I keep doing things wrong, failing to be what He wants me to be, and still He lovingly works in my life. What a wonderful God!

Thankful for a patient husband and a patient God,

Gloria

Something to Think About

If God is so patient with us when we do wrong, shouldn't we respond to others in the same way?

Prayer

Father, thank you for being so patient with me. I commit myself to being patient with others.

My Thoughts

Mind Changer

Why is it everything good for you tastes bad and everything bad for you tastes good? That may be a slight exaggeration, but only slight!

When was the last time you expounded on how wonderful a stalk of celery tasted? A piece of Mississippi Mud Cake, now that's another story!

People say once you start eating healthy foods you won't want to eat all that junk food. Right! It's going to take some serious mind changing for me to prefer a carrot stick over a Reese's Peanut Butter Cup, a head of cabbage over a hot fudge sundae, or tofu over strawberries dipped in chocolate.

I know it's better to eat healthy foods. I really am trying. It has been weeks since I've had a hot fudge sundae. I did cheat and have a small Reese's Peanut Butter Cup. Does it help that I felt badly after I ate it?

I'm longing for the day when I feel like those healthy people. They would gag at the thought of a hot fudge sundae and *never* pollute their bodies with a Reese's Peanut Butter Cup. Some day. Some day.

My spiritual life often parallels my physical life. The Bible tells me there are things that are good for me and things I need to eliminate from my life. While I know that to be true, it's not always easy to do! It is only as I allow God to change my spiritual appetite that I become spiritually healthy.

Praying I allow God to make me spiritually healthy,

Gloria

Something to Think About

Are you as concerned about your spiritual health as you are about your physical health?

Prayer

God, help me concentrate on being spiritually healthy.

Amen.

My Thoughts

Butter Is Not Better

I left groceries in my husband's car on Friday. On Sunday, he mentioned he had seen the bags in his car and wondered if anything was perishable. How would I know? I did that on Friday and it was now Sunday. Really, what does the man expect of me?

I grabbed the bags and began walking across the parking lot to my car. I happened to look down. A liquid from one of the bags was oozing onto my slacks. I stopped and looked to see what the liquid was. I had two pounds of melted butter dripping from the bag!

I looked back. Unlike Hansel and Gretel who had a left a trail of breadcrumbs, I had left a trail of butter.

As I rushed to the car and fumbled for my keys, I dropped my Bible and purse in the butter-filled bag!

I threw everything into the car, grabbed some paper towels, and went back to remove my butter trail. I didn't want anyone slipping because of my neglect.

So, there I was in ninety-five-degree weather, trying to wipe butter off the sidewalk. I'm sure the church people wanted to know what I was doing but were afraid to ask!

I wonder what kind of trail I'm leaving for my children, my grandchildren, my friends, and my church family. Is it something that will be beneficial for them or will it be something that makes them slip along life's road?

Praying I leave a trail of godliness for those who come after me,

Gloria

Something to Think About

Everyone will leave a trail. What kind of trail will yours be?

Prayer

Father, help me live my life in such a way that those who come after me will not slip because of the trail I have left for them.

Amen.

My Thoughts

Getting Out of the House

As I'm aging, getting ready to go out of the house takes longer.

First, I have to put on moisturizer. It's supposed to make my skin plump up. Unfortunately, the only thing plump I see in the mirror is my body!

Next, there's eye cream for the crow's feet. I don't know when, but those crows have surely been walking around on my face a lot!

Now comes foundation. My foundation is crumbling pretty badly and I fear nothing is going to be able to prop it up again.

Eye shadow is next. It's supposed to make it less obvious that my eyelids are sagging. I don't think it's working!

I now put on mascara. It does help, but barely. At least you don't have to get a microscope to see I have eyelashes!

The final thing is lipstick. I now buy the permanent kind. Of course, when I put it on, I have to construct a new line on one side of my lips so it will match the other side. I cheat a little to make my lips look fuller. My hips may not have shrunk, but my lips have! Two hours have now passed. I'm ready to face the world . . . sort of.

Funny how we're willing to spend so much time working on the outside and so little time working on the inside. That's where real beauty comes from, and that kind of beauty doesn't fade!

Praying the beauty of Jesus can be seen in me,

Gloria

Something to Think About

Which is more important to you, outer beauty or inner beauty? Inner beauty is eternal.

Prayer

God, I don't want to be more concerned about what I look like on the outside than I am about inward beauty. Help me yield to your beauty treatment.

Amen.

My Thoughts

Big-Brained Grandchildren

Yesterday I took my seven-year-old grandson to a movie. On the way there, we stopped at the grocery store.

His family eats mostly organic food and he is allergic to gluten so I picked up a box of organic, gluten-free cereal. I, on the other hand, chose some Sugary Sweet Full of Junk That Will Taste Just Like You're Eating Candy cereal. Well, it wasn't *really* that bad!

When we got home, I told my husband I had bought the organic cereal, but I couldn't remember the name of it. My grandson (remember, he's only seven) quickly told his Paw Paw the name of the cereal.

He then turned to me, laughed, and said, "Nanny, I think my brain is bigger than yours." My seven-year-old grandson thinks he's smarter than me? That was a little hard to take. While it may be true, it surely does hurt to hear it!

I don't like the idea, but I guess I'll have to live with the fact that *all* my grandchildren probably feel they have bigger brains than their grandmother. See what being forgetful can do to your self-esteem!

While they may think their Nanny has a small brain, I hope they think she has a big heart!

Thanking God for big-brained grandchildren,

Gloria

Something to Think About

Do those you love think you have a big heart that is open to God? We can get by with small brains, but big hearts open to God are vital.

Prayer

Father, I'm not so concerned with the size of my brain. I am concerned with the size of my heart. Help me be willing to let you give me a heart as big as yours.

Amen.

My Thoughts

Myth Buster

Have you ever seen the television show called *Mythbusters*? Each week the hosts take something everyone believes to be true and tries to see if it is fact or a myth. Although I'm not on television, *I* am a myth buster.

Are you familiar with the old adage, "Smoke follows beauty"? It means if you're beautiful and near a fire, the smoke will naturally blow in your direction.

I've heard that statement since I was a kid. Until now, I believed it. Why shouldn't I? Well, I don't believe it anymore!

It's confirmed. It's a myth. Smoke *does not* always follow beauty! How do I know?

On a recent camping trip with friends, we built a campfire. The smoke from the fire followed me everywhere I stood. If I went to the right, it came to the right. If I went to the left, it went to the left. I just couldn't get away from it!

Hey, I look in the mirror. To say what stares back me is a beauty is more far-fetched than a science-fiction movie!

I just thought of something. Not one of my friends commented that the smoke was following me. They're old enough to know the saying. I think I should be insulted!

Although I've debunked the myth that smoke follows beauty, I do know something that follows me. I read it in a book. A special book.

The Bible says, "Goodness and mercy shall follow me all the days of my life" (Psalm 23:6a KJV). Hey, I'd rather have that following me anyway!

Thanking God for his goodness and mercy,

Gloria

Something to Think About

When is the last time you thanked God for His goodness and mercy toward you?

Prayer

God, thank you that your goodness and mercy follow me all the days of my life. I don't deserve it, but I do appreciate it.

Amen.

My Thoughts

Old Age Approaching

Lots of things change as we women grow older. We get beards. We get bad knees. We get bad hips.

As our downward spiral continues, we can't hear, we can't see, and we can't smell.

I'm getting closer to old age. Some think I'm already there.

I'm trying to prepare for the old-age stage of my life.

I'm buying up eyeglasses in various strengths. The last step will be to purchase a magnifying glass.

I don't know about the beard thing. If people start saying, "Hey, mister," I may have to purchase a man's shaver.

I think I'll load up on those nose sprays that are supposed to open up your sinuses. Maybe they will help when I lose my sense of smell.

Did I mention getting older takes money? Lots of money. I need to start saving now for future hearing aids, hip and knee replacements, and medicine.

Old age can be depressing . . . or not. It all depends on our attitude. We don't have to allow things to get us down. We *choose to.*

We can consider each day as a gift from God or a burden to bear. Admittedly, sometimes it's not easy to see the day as a gift. Yet, it's in the difficult times that we need to rejoice the most.

Rejoicing takes our minds off our troubles, our aches, and our frustrations. So no matter what your age or your condition, rejoice today!

"Rejoice in the Lord always; and again I say, rejoice!" (Philippians 4:4 KJV).

Choosing to rejoice, even when it is difficult,

Gloria

Something to Think About

Is the Devil trying to make you believe getting older will mean you cannot have a full and meaningful life?

Prayer

God, help me appreciate whatever stage of life I am in, and live it to the fullest.

Amen.

My Thoughts

Mirrors

Some days I like having a full-length mirror in my bedroom. Other days, I hate it.

Recently I did what those diet books tell you to do. You know, stand in front of the mirror naked and look at your body to see areas you want to work on. I will *never* subject myself to that again! I'll just note that all areas are in need of repair and let it go at that.

Maybe I could break my mirror up into tiny little pieces and make one of those disco balls that turns round and round and makes reflections on the wall. No, that might keep me awake at night.

Or, how about if I never clean the mirror? That way, it will become so smudged that there is no possibility I will be able to get a good view when I stand in front of it. I don't think my husband would appreciate that. He has enough to deal with being married to me. One more thing might put him over the edge.

I could give my mirror away. But why would I want to subject another person to what I have gone through?

I guess the only solution is to change my thinking patterns. When I look in the mirror and think I see Mrs. Frump, I'll just tell myself, "Gloria, according to the Scripture, you are fearfully and wonderfully made."

When I'm standing next to a woman who looks like she just stepped out of a fashion magazine, I may even have to repeat "fearfully and wonderfully made" several times. If I keep at it, I believe I'll be able to change my thinking patterns!

When God looks at me, He thinks I'm beautiful. Don't all fathers think their kids are adorable? How awesome to think that the God of the universe looks at me and sees beauty! I need to see myself as He sees me.

"I am fearfully and wonderfully made. I am fearfully and wonderfully made . . . "

Gloria

Something to Think About

Are you aware that your worth has nothing to do with your external appearance?

Prayer

Father, help me remember my worth is not based on what I look like, but on being your child.

Amen.

My Thoughts

Managing Mayhem

I was getting ready for church. Unlike my regular wait-till-the-last-minute philosophy, I actually started a bit earlier. Maybe I took a longer shower or brushed my teeth a few extra minutes because, when I looked at the clock, I realized I had to hurry to get to church on time.

As I was putting on my makeup, I dropped mascara on the front of my white blouse. I tried to scrub the mascara off with soap and water—too bad I had chosen the waterproof kind! It didn't come off, but it did make a round black circle on my blouse. I didn't have time to change, so I decided I would have to wear one black polka dot on my blouse.

I rushed out and started to put my foot, which was inside an open-toed shoe, into the car. I noticed a very large run in my knee-high stocking (I *never* wear pantyhose anymore). I grabbed the knee-high, pulled it forward a few inches, and tucked it back under my foot. I imagined it coming loose and flapping each time I took a step.

I planned to finish putting on my makeup in the car. I pulled out of the driveway and grabbed for my makeup case. *No case!*

When I got to church, I rushed into my Bible study class and reached for my Bible. *No Bible!*

A friend handed me a Bible out of the cabinet. I reached into my purse to get my glasses. *No glasses!*

If I could have held the Bible between my toes, I may have been able to see the words! But I couldn't do that without my knee-high flapping.

Concentrating on the mishaps could have made me miss out on the blessings of studying God's Word and fellowshipping with believers. What a waste that would have been.

Trying to concentrate on the right things,

Gloria

Something to Think About

Are you letting hectic days or mishaps interfere with your worship of God?

Prayer

God, I have so many hectic days. Help me not let them interfere with my worship of you.

Amen.

My Thoughts

Pots, Spoons, and No-Fail Sauce

I feel if you have to cook, then get it over with as soon as possible. Forget all the cooking shows that say, "Put on medium heat." Me? I crank the fire up as high as it will go. Unfortunately, there are varying results from such an action.

Once I was making some no-fail hot fudge sauce from a recipe my friend had given me. I questioned the no-fail thing, but she assured me I could *not* fail with this. Ha! Did I fool her.

I had guests over and decided to wow them with sundaes made with homemade hot fudge. I put the sauce on the stove, cranked the heat as high as it would go, and stirred the sauce with a wooden spoon that I left in the pot. I then proceeded outside to entertain my guests. Quite some time later, I remembered the hot fudge sauce. I rushed inside. Too late!

On my stove sat a pot with a black, brick-like concoction inside. I tried to lift the spoon out. As I did, the entire pot rose. My guests had hot fudge sundaes without the hot fudge!

I tried everything to get that spoon out and clean the pot. As we say about marriage, "the two had become one." I had to throw them both in the trash. My only consolation was I had one less pot and spoon to wash!

Did that teach me a lesson? Yes. Did I apply it to my life? No. Years have passed since that incident and I am still burning things. I've even convinced my husband the brown, crunchy pieces he finds in his rice really are supposed to be there.

Like me, do you have areas in your life you stubbornly refuse to change? Refusing to lower the heat will only result in burned pots and food. Failing to change in our spiritual lives has greater consequences. By the way, I have a great recipe for *almost* no-fail hot fudge sauce.

Trying to apply the lessons I learn,

Gloria

Something to Think About

Are you willing to apply to your life the lessons God teaches you?

Prayer

Father, I want to apply to my life the things you teach me.

Amen.

My Thoughts

Spiritual DNA

They say you are what you eat. I hope that isn't true. If it is, you might notice me looking like a chilidog.

When I was younger, I looked forward to the fair each year so I could indulge in *carnie* food. After I married, my husband was always amazed that I could eat all that junk and not get sick. He called me "old iron gut."

Years have passed and I don't think the old gut is made of iron anymore. More like aluminum foil.

Chili dogs don't set well like they once did and it seems they don't taste quite as good as when I was younger. Still, every now and then, I indulge in one.

I have a friend who eats almost nothing that has fat in it; no cheese, no fries, and no fatty meats. She says the sight of all that fat actually makes her queasy. Why? Because she has changed her pattern of eating.

My eating patterns are changing. So are my living patterns. Things I wanted to do before just don't appeal to me as they once did. That's because I now have God's spiritual DNA.

As I allow God to live his life out through me, I don't desire to do things that are contrary to his nature. In fact, they may make me a little queasy.

Glad my spiritual DNA has been changed,

Gloria

Something to Think About

Has your spiritual DNA been changed? Living patterns change because we are new creations.

Prayer

God, thank you for saving me from my sins and changing my spiritual DNA.

Amen.

My Thoughts

Not Without a Fight!

It's that time I *hate*. I put it off as much as I can. What is it? Going to the doctor for a mammogram? Having a tooth pulled? No. Something I hate more. Well, maybe not more than a mammogram! The dreaded thing I have to face this morning is coloring my hair.

Some of you are growing old gracefully. Me, I'm going down kicking and screaming!

My husband says he's doing the growing old gracefully bit. He's not going to shame me into doing the same. Men can do that because older men with gray hair look distinguished. Women with gray hair, well, they just look old.

Actually, I'm not sure what color my hair is. I've not seen the original in a long time. If the roots are any indication, *Snow White and the Seven Dwarfs* comes to mind.

I'll continue to try to hide my aging process by coloring my hair. I'm even threatening after-life visitations to my family if they lay me in the casket with my white roots showing!

So, I'm sitting here before my computer, my white towel with brown blotches wrapped around my shoulders. Its purpose is to catch any errant solution that might want to color other areas of my body. Only you at-home hair coloring ladies can get the picture here.

I expect to be transformed into a brown-haired beauty. I exaggerated on the last part of that sentence. Some things can only be changed with plastic surgery, and I'm not sure that would even help!

The Bible says God knows us so intimately that He could tell us how many hairs are on our heads. Don't you find it amazing that the great Creator of the universe bothers to know that? One thing is for sure. I'm going to see that He's the only one who knows the color of each of those hairs!

Thankful God knows me so well,

Gloria

Something to Think About

If God knows such a minute thing as the very number of hairs on our head, can we doubt He cares about all aspects of our life?

Prayer

Father, thank you that you know me so intimately. Help me desire to know you as intimately as you know me.

Amen.

My Thoughts

Droopy Eyelids

I've got another thing to deal with about growing older. The problem is droopy eyelids. They're sagging so much I'm thinking it won't be too long before they blur my eyesight. I know everything else sags as we get older, but does it have to include eyelids too?

I can use a little dark shadow to try to hide the eyelid landslide, but that doesn't help the fact that they are about to cover my eyes. I knew your eyesight worsened as you got older. I just didn't realize it was because your eyelids had slipped!

Since I can't afford plastic surgery to remedy the situation, I'm trying to think up an alternative. I considered propping my eyelids up with toothpicks, but thought that might be painful.

I bought some crazy glue the other day. Maybe I can put a dab on the top of my eyelid, pull the sagging skin up, and glue it in place. The only problem is, I'm afraid I'll wind up with permanently open eyes. Then I'll have another problem.

I guess I'll let the eyelids sag. When they get past my eyes, I'll just have to read standing on my head so the sags won't get in my way. This old-age business is a real challenge!

Life is full of challenges no matter what our age. Some days I rise above my challenges. I think God and I can conquer anything. Other days, I wonder if God has forgotten me. Deep down, I know He hasn't, but the challenges seem heavier, harder to bear. I question if I'll be able to rise above them.

God is faithful. I find I survive one day, then another, and another. Just like He knew I could. You can do the same!

Thankful for a God who is with me in all my challenges,

Gloria

Something to Think About

Are you confident God only allows things into your life that He is sure you can handle?

Prayer

God, I choose to believe you will never put anything into my life that you do not first give me the strength to handle.

Amen.

My Thoughts

Questions for God

I woke up at 4:15 this morning. I wanted to sleep longer but I have a sleep disorder. It's called menopause. I thought I would be over it by now, but, lucky me, I'm still in the throes of it.

I want to ask God about menopause when I get to heaven. I want to ask him why men don't have this *pause*. I also wonder why it is called *men*-o-pause.

Why do I burst into tears for no apparent reason?

Why do I wake up sweating like I've run a marathon and find myself throwing off the covers only to be grabbing those same covers a few minutes later because I'm freezing?

Why do I sometimes have a Jekyll and Hyde personality? Sweet as Milk Duds one minute, sour as unprocessed olives the next?

Why do I have trouble remembering what I walked into a room for?

Getting older has other changes. Knees ache. Hearing goes. Eyesight dwindles. Have I depressed you sufficiently?

I'm not saying I am older. I'm still a thirty-year-old inside—I started to put *twenty,* but that would have been stretching it a bit too much. It's just my outside, the one I see in the mirror, that belies the inside.

I wonder if God made our bodies deteriorate so we would desire to leave this old world and be with Him. If we were robust and life held no difficulty, would we really want to die and go to heaven?

I'll accept the fact that God has a purpose in this plan of deterioration. But, I'm still going to ask Him about it when I get to heaven!

Trusting the wisdom of God,

Gloria

Something to Think About

Are you trusting God's wisdom? It's easy when all is going well, not so easy when you are suffering.

Prayer

God, help me have confidence that you never make mistakes so whatever is happening in my life is for my good.

Amen.

My Thoughts

Diets and Believing Lies

Isn't it funny how we try to fool ourselves into believing something is right when we know it isn't? I know that truth from experience!

My husband's brother and his wife came to visit us. The brother was on a diet. It was a diet I'd never heard of, and believe me: I knew most every one that had come out in the last forty years!

He told me all you had to do was drink some grapefruit juice with any food you ate. The grapefruit juice was supposed to do something in your body that negated lots of the calories you ate. The pounds were guaranteed to melt away. You could even eat all the chocolate you wanted as long as you drank the grapefruit juice. This was the diet I had been waiting for all my life! I decided to go on it with him.

We took our guests camping. As we traveled, my brother-in-law and I would grab our big bars of chocolate. I'm talkin' *big* here, the kind that could feed a family of eight. We would snap off a giant chunk of chocolate, take a swig of grapefruit juice, and savor our chocolate fix.

I'm not sure how many chocolate bars we ate on our trip. The large trash bag full of chocolate wrappers made me believe it was quite a few.

When I got home, I rushed to my scales to see how much weight I had lost. I had gained five pounds. Thank goodness we weren't gone for several weeks or I would have had to buy bigger clothes!

Deep down in my heart, I felt the diet didn't make sense. It went against all logic. But because I wanted that chocolate, I chose to believe a lie.

We can have the same illogical reasoning in our spiritual lives. We instinctively know when we shouldn't do something, say something, think something, or feel something. It goes against the cautions of the Holy Spirit and our nagging conscience.

Since we want to do it, we refuse to heed the cautions. Doing that is far more serious than yielding to a chocolate bar.

Hoping today I don't fool myself into believing wrong is right,

Gloria

Something to Think About

The Holy Spirit will always direct you into truth. Are you willing to listen?

Prayer

Father, reveal to me when I am trying to justify wrongs I want to do. Give me courage to do what I know is right.

Amen.

My Thoughts

My New Book

I have an idea for a new book. I think it might sell. It will be titled *Life after the Big Fifty: And You Thought the Forties Were Rough!*

I know I'll need catchy chapter titles. I've been thinking about that. Here are a few I'm considering:

- Help! Everything Has Fallen and I Can't Get It Back Up!
- Wrinkled Sheets and My Face: A Comparison
- Depends Commercials: No Laughing Matter
- What Jiggles Like Jell-O but Isn't?
- Mirror, Mirror on the Wall, Why I Hate You Most of All

Do you think it has potential?

We complain about aging, but it does have some great advantages. It quickens the time when we will shed these old bodies. The rewards of that will be:

- Going to heaven;
- Bodies that don't wear out;
- Being united with loved ones; and
- Seeing God the Father and Jesus our Savior. I saved the best for last!

Thankful aging brings me closer to all the joys of heaven,

Gloria

Something to Think About

Are you letting the promises of heaven banish any fear of aging and dying?

Prayer

God, thank You I don't have to fear aging or death because You have prepared a wonderful place for me to live with You eternally.

Amen.

My Thoughts

Underwear and Brain Wiring

When God created me, I think there was a short circuit in my brain. I can't remember anything past a few minutes, sometimes a few seconds. I don't think it's Alzheimer's disease. I've had it since childhood.

What kid do you know who forgets to put on her underwear before she goes to school? Yep. You read it right. I went to school without my underwear. Didn't even know it until I had to go to the restroom.

After the potty break, I prayed all day there would be no wind to raise my skirt and the fourteen starched slips I had underneath. I walked funny the rest of the day. It's not easy keeping your legs together while you walk. You try it!

Over the years, I have forgotten a slip or two, but never the underwear. I *have* checked a few times when out because I couldn't remember if I had put it on or not.

My forgetfulness is getting worse as I get older. I'll be talking and my thoughts go hide somewhere in my brain and dare me to find them. I'll go into a room and then wonder why on earth I am there.

The worst is when I'm teaching my Bible study class and am about to say something when I realize the words I had planned to say have floated away into the gray matter. I am left with a blank stare on my face. My class has learned my look of desperation and always tries to make suggestions on what I might have wanted to say.

I keep telling myself God does all things well, even when He created me. After all, my husband and children would have had a very dull existence had they not had to put up with me all these years. I just hope *they* believe God does all things well!

Believing God does . . . now, what was I going to say?

Gloria

Something to Think About

Are you aware God made no mistakes when He created you? He has a purpose and plan for your life.

Prayer

God, help me accept that you did not make any mistakes when you created me.

Amen.

My Thoughts

Clean Kitchens and Clean Lives

I've hit another milestone in my life. Not a big one in the eyes of most, but a really, really big one for me. For over twenty-one days, I have cleaned my kitchen in the evening. Yeah for me!

You neat and tidy types may be saying, "What's so big about that? Doesn't everybody always clean the kitchen after dinner?" Well, I want to open your eyes. *No, they do not!* At least I'm hoping I'm not the only one who has left a sink full of dishes because I just didn't have the energy (or desire) to wash them.

Now I feel good when I walk into my kitchen in the morning and find everything nice and neat. The only thing I hate is we have to mess it up again! I do that as seldom as possible by convincing my husband we should have breakfast . . . or lunch . . . or dinner out. I have been known to convince him to do all three in a day, but not as often as I would like!

Another thing that makes me feel good is when I am able to clean up my life by winning a victory over some sin. It's especially nice when my life has been cleaned up in an area that's been dirty for some time.

If I want to have a clean life, I have to seek daily the power of the Holy Spirit to rid my flesh of those things that make it "dirty." I do that by listening to the Holy Spirit's prompting. He does not speak audibly, but if I pay attention, I can hear Him guiding me to do what is right.

I need to develop the spiritual habit of letting the Holy Spirit control my life.

Happy to have a clean kitchen, but happier I can have a clean life,

Gloria

Something to Think About

Is there evidence in your life that it is being cleaned up? It can only be done by yielding to the Holy Spirit.

Prayer

Father, I yield my life to the Holy Spirit and ask that He clean up my life and make me conformed to the image of Jesus.

Amen.

My Thoughts

Making God Look Good

As I started into the eight o'clock church service to read Scripture and lead in prayer, I realized I didn't have my notes. I was fearful I had left them at home. I ran to my car as fast as someone my age can, trying not to knock people down as I went. The notes were on the seat of the car. Hallelujah!

After a few minutes of gasping for breath, I rushed back inside. Unfortunately, all that running necessitated a bathroom stop. I hurriedly, well, you know what I did. No need going into too much detail!

As I rushed out of the bathroom, I happened to look down. I am so happy I did! My slacks were unzipped *and* unbuttoned. I retreated into the bathroom and fixed things.

I rushed onto the platform, read the Scripture, and prayed without another hitch. Despite all I had been through, God blessed. Another crazy morning survived!

On extremely difficult days, I pray and ask God to give me strength to handle my problems in the right way. I want people to see my heavenly Father can sustain me through any difficulty.

It's not always easy to handle difficulties in the right way, but when I do, I make God look good. And, it makes me feel good, too.

Hoping my actions always make God look good,

Gloria

Something to Think About

How you handle difficulties should be what distinguishes between you and non-Christians. Are your actions making God look good?

Prayer

Father, I want to handle my difficulties in such a way that I make you look good so others will be drawn to you.

Amen.

My Thoughts

Squandering Time

I've always heard that older people go to bed earlier and get up earlier than young people. That may be a problem for me. I have always gone to bed early. By the time I'm eighty, I may be crawling under the covers about one in the afternoon!

I like getting up early. If I don't, I feel I have wasted too much of my day. Time I can never recover.

When I wake up early, I spend time reading the Bible and praying. I also write early in the morning before the afternoon brain fog sets in. I do my yard work in the early morning cool. You notice I said nothing about cleaning the house. I hate doing that no matter what time I get up!

Have you ever thought about lost time? I have. I've wondered if I've squandered it. Were there times I should have done something but didn't? Have I done things that were not worth wasting precious time on?

I suppose all of us could look back and find some period in which we wish we had used our time more wisely. That can be good if it spurs us on to change our patterns. It can be bad if we let the Devil drag us into despair about it.

While I may have squandered my time in the past, I do not have to continue doing so. It's a choice I make.

Hoping I'm not squandering the time God has given me,

Gloria

Something to Think About

The Bible tells us God has allotted each of us a designated amount of time. How are you using your allotted time?

Prayer

God, show me how to use wisely the time you have given me.

Amen.

My Thoughts

The Books and *The Book*

I need to get more light in my bedroom. Either that or wear my glasses when I get dressed. Today is a good example of why I need to see better.

I was getting ready to meet my husband for lunch—he hasn't eaten lunch at home for ages—and the last thing I put on was my shoes. I probably wouldn't have noticed that I had on two different shoes if I hadn't walked kind of funny when I started to leave. My right leg seemed to be longer than the left and I walked with a limp.

When I looked down to try to figure out what the problem was, I realized I had on two different kinds of shoes. The limp was caused by the fact that one shoe had a higher heel than the other!

It was then I noticed the toe of one shoe was pointed and the other was square! At least I realized it before I rushed out the door. This time, only I knew my silliness. It's for sure my friends don't need another thing to add to the list of ding-a-ling things I have done.

Jesus had a list about me, too. The Bible says this list was written in *the books*, books that reveal the sins of all the people who have ever lived. A wonderful thing happened when Jesus saved me from my sins. My name was taken out of *the books* and put in *the* book, the Book of Life.

All those horrible things listed about me were erased. I will *never* have to face them. Jesus took them to the cross. Hallelujah, what a Savior!

Thankful all my wrong deeds have been erased from *the books*,

Gloria

Something to Think About

Having your name listed in the Book of Life determines your eternal destiny. Is yours listed there?

Prayer

Father, thank You for providing a way for all my sins to be forgiven so that my name can be written in the Book of Life and I can live with you in heaven.

My Thoughts

Conclusion

All women, no matter how perfect they seem to us, have flaws. Perfection is only a facade.

However, there is coming a day when we can be perfect. That day is when Jesus returns to take His children home to live with Him forever in a perfect place called heaven. I look forward to that perfection!

Are you God's child? You can be. Here's how:

1. Acknowledge Jesus died in your place to pay for your sins.
2. Confess that you are a sinner.
3. Ask Jesus to forgive you of your sins and come into your life to be your Savior and Lord.

Suggested prayer to receive Jesus as your Savior and Lord.

> God, I know I'm not perfect. I know I've sinned. I believe Jesus died on the cross to take away my sins. I believe He rose from the grave to break the power of sin and death. I ask you to forgive me of my sins. Come into my life and take control. Thank you for saving me from my sins.
>
> Amen.

If you prayed that prayer, you became a child of God. Welcome to the family!

If you asked Jesus into your heart and would like a booklet to help you as you begin your exciting journey as God's child, contact me at gloriamcqueenstockstill@gmail.com.

Blessings,

Gloria

About the Author

Gloria McQueen Stockstill lives in Southern California with her husband, Wayne. She has authored four retold Bible story books, English and Spanish, and has written for Focus on the Family's Clubhouse Jr. magazine as well as other publications. She is a curriculum writer for a Christian school.

Gloria has led state and national conferences for her denomination as well as Bible studies, small group presentations, and retreats for churches. She was a member of the National Advisory Committee for Women in Evangelism, Southern Baptist Convention.

CPSIA information can be obtained at www.ICGtesting.com
Printed in the USA
LVOW111931010612

284264LV00003B/2/P